MOVING WATER CAN BE USED FOR ENERGY

Energy

MELISSA GISH

CREATIVE EDUCATION

Published by Creative Education

123 South Broad Street, Mankato, Minnesota 56001

Creative Education is an imprint of The Creative Company

Designed by Rita Marshall

Photographs by Corbis (Paul Barton, Bettmann, W. Cody, George B. Diebold, Darrell

Gulin), Getty Images (Nat Farhman, Lester Lefkowitz, Nicholas Rigg, Pascal Rondeau),

Tom Stack and Associates

Cover illustration © 1996 Roberto Innocenti

Printed in the United States of America

Library of Congress Cataloging-in-Publication Data

Gish, Melissa. Energy / by Melissa Gish.

p. cm. — (My first look at science)

ISBN 1-58341-372-3

1. Power resources—Juvenile literature. I. Title. II. Series.

TJ163.23.G57 2004   531'.6—dc22   2004058256

First edition 9 8 7 6 5 4 3 2 1

ENERGY

ENERGY FROM THE SUN

Everything on Earth has energy. Energy is what makes things move. It can change from one form to another. Some forms of energy come from nature.

The sun is hot. It makes a special kind of energy. We call it solar energy. This energy helps all living things grow. Plants change solar energy into food. Snakes and lizards change solar energy into body heat.

TREES GET ENERGY TO GROW FROM THE SUN

Some people use solar energy to heat houses and run TVs and computers. Special **panels** catch the sun's heat. This heat is turned into a new form of energy called electricity.

ENERGY WORKS FOR US

People need energy to run factories, farms, and cities. Rivers and wind have energy we can use. They can make things move. Windmills use the wind to make energy.

Special buildings called
power plants make electricity.
They send it out through wires.

Waterwheels in a river make energy, too. This energy can be stored in **batteries**.

We need energy to make cars and trucks go. This energy comes from things we call fuel. Gas, oil, and coal are all kinds of fuel. We call them fossil fuels. They formed in the ground a long, long time ago. People dig in the ground to get fossil fuels. Then they are burned to make heat or electricity.

Light is called

"radiant" energy.

It spreads out, or "radiates,"

in many directions.

OIL IS FOUND DEEP UNDER THE GROUND

Energy in Your Body

Your body needs energy to live and grow. It gets this energy from food. If you do not eat breakfast, you may feel weak. Your body is telling you that it needs energy.

LIFTING HEAVY WEIGHTS TAKES LOTS OF ENERGY

FOOD GIVES US THE ENERGY TO RUN AND PLAY

Energy is moving all through your body. Even when you are standing still, you are using energy. When you run around, you use more energy. When you throw a ball, some of the energy from your body goes into the ball. This is what makes the ball move.

Albert Einstein was a

scientist who studied energy.

He was one of the smartest

people ever.

ENERGY EVERYWHERE

Energy cannot be made or destroyed. It just moves around and changes form. Movement is a kind of energy. So is sound. Heat and light are forms of energy, too.

Even things that do not move have energy. A rock has energy that is used if it falls or is dropped. If the rock does not move, its energy is not used.

EVERYTHING HAS ENERGY—EVEN ROCKS

Energy can move from place to place. There are lots of times when we cannot see energy, but it is moving. The energy called electricity travels through wires. Sound energy travels through the air when we shout. Energy is everywhere!

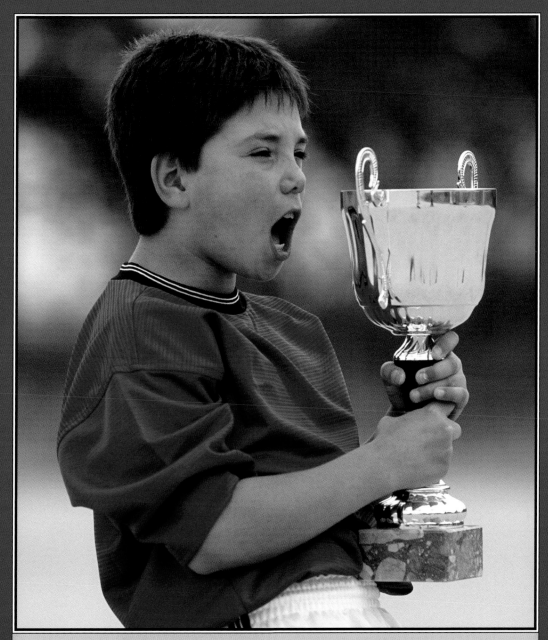

SHOUTING MAKES ENERGY CALLED SOUND ENERGY

Hands-on: Energy at Work

You can see energy at work with this experiment.

What You Need

Two marbles

Stairs that do not have carpet

What You Do

1. Put one marble on the bottom step. Give it a gentle push. Watch how far it rolls when it hits the floor.
2. Put the other marble on a higher step. Give it a gentle push. Watch how far it rolls when it hits the floor.

The second marble should roll farther than the first one. Objects that are higher off the ground have more energy waiting to be used.

PUSHING A MARBLE GIVES IT ENERGY

Index

Words to Know

batteries—containers that store energy for later use

panels—flat objects that soak up sunshine

scientist—a person who does experiments to learn about science

waterwheel—a round object that is turned when water moves over it

Read More

Adams, Richard C. *Energy Projects for Young Scientists*. New York: Franklin Watts, 2002.

Bradley, Kimberly Brubaker, and Paul Meisel. *Energy Makes Things Happen*. New York: HarperCollins, 2003.

Hewitt, Sally. *Full of Energy*. New York: Children's Press, 1998.

Explore the Web

Dr. E's Energy Lab http://www.eere.energy.gov/kids

Energy Chasers http://www.exelonenergy.com/kids

Energy Quest: Science Projects http://www.energyquest.ca.gov/projects